BODYWORKS

nose

Katherine Goode

BLACKBIRCH PRESS, INC.
WOODBRIDGE, CONNECTICUT

To Dr. Paul Goodman, with thanks

Published by Blackbirch Press, Inc.
260 Amity Road
Woodbridge, CT 06525

e-mail: staff@blackbirch.com
web site: www.blackbirch.com

Text copyright ©Katherine Goode 1999

©2000 by Blackbirch Press, Inc.
First U.S. Edition

Printed in Hong Kong

First published 1999 by
MACMILLAN EDUCATION AUSTRALIA PTY LTD
627 Chapel Street, South Yarra 3141

10 9 8 7 6 5 4 3 2 1

Photo Credits:
Cover photo: ©Dick Smolinski
Pages 24, 26: Austral International; page 14: Australian Picture Library/©Peter Menzel; page 27: Coo-ee Picture Library; pages 6, 7, 12: Graham Meadows; pages 8, 15, 20, 22, 23, 28: Great Southern Stock; page 11: International Photo Library; pages 1, 4, 18, 19, 21, 23, 25, 28, 29, 30: The Picture Source.

Library of Congress Cataloging-in-Publication Data
Goode, Katherine, 1949–
Nose / by Katherine Goode.
    p.   cm. — (Bodyworks)
    Includes index.
    Summary: Explains the functions of the different parts of the nose.
    ISBN 1-56711-493-8 (hardcover : alk. paper)
    1. Nose—Juvenile literature. [1. Nose.] I. Title.
QP458.G66   2000
612.8'6—dc21   00-008126
                                                      CIP

Contents

The nose

Your nose helps you to breathe and allows you to smell. It also helps to make the sound of your voice.

Noses have many different shapes and sizes.
They can be big or small, flat or pointed,
straight or crooked.

Parts of the nose

The bridge of your nose contains **elastic tissue** and bone. It gives your nose its shape.

bridge

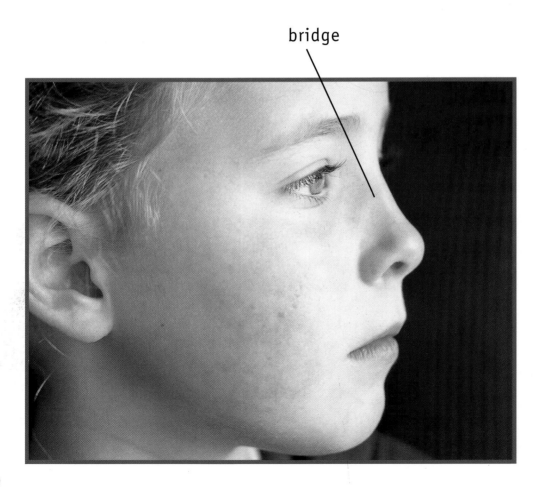

At the tip, your nose is soft and movable.
The nostrils are the 2 openings at the end of
your nose.

Inside your nostrils there are short, coarse hairs. They keep tiny pieces of dust or flower pollen from entering your body. Your nostrils lead to 2 tunnels inside your nose. These tunnels are called nasal passages.

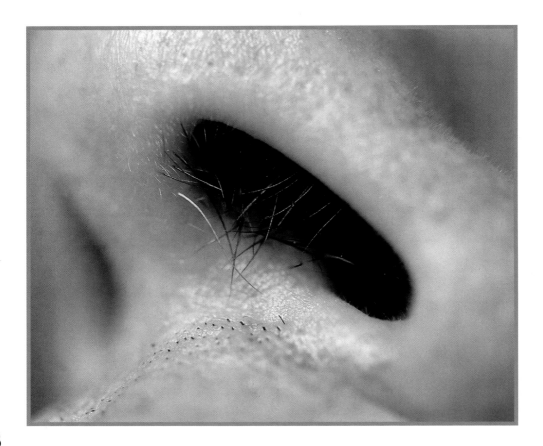

Your nasal passages are covered with soft, moist **mucous tissues**, which make **mucus**. The mucus traps dust pieces and flower pollen.

Your nasal passages are separated by elastic, bony walls.

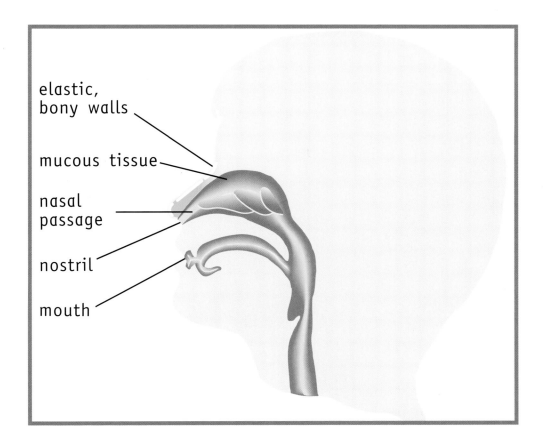

elastic,
bony walls

mucous tissue

nasal
passage

nostril

mouth

Breathing

When you breathe in, air enters your nostrils and goes up the nasal passages. The nasal passages warm and moisten the air. Air passes through the back of your throat, down your windpipe, and into your lungs.

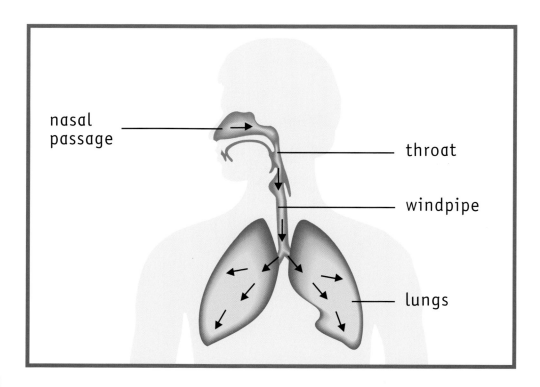

nasal passage

throat

windpipe

lungs

Your nose reacts to changes in temperature. If you go outside on a cold day, your nose senses that the air is cold and dry. Your nose then produces more moisture in the mucous tissues in order to protect your nose. If you then go into a warm room, your nose will have too much moisture, and it will become runny.

Smell

Food, plants, animals, and many other things give off odors. When you smell an odor, the air containing the odor travels up your nostrils. Small **nerves** inside your nose send messages to your brain.

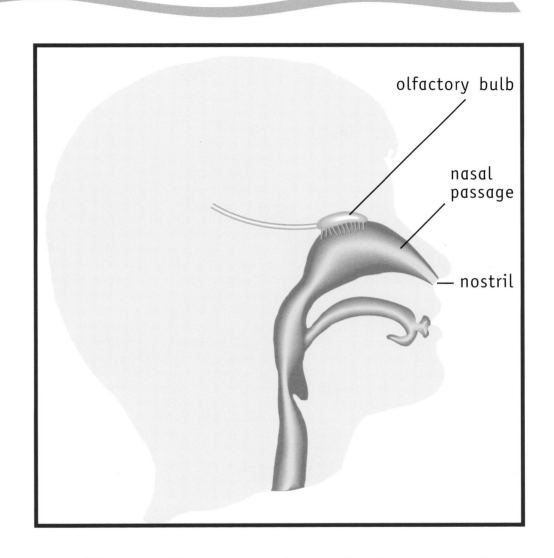

olfactory bulb

nasal passage

nostril

An olfactory (having to do with the sense of smell) bulb sits on top of each nasal passage. It is a part of the brain. It has nerves that sense smell.

Your sense of smell is closely related to your sense of taste.

If you shut your eyes and hold your nose while you are eating, you will find that it is hard to taste food.

The sinuses

The sinuses are spaces in the bones of your skull that are connected to the nasal passages. They are filled with air and act as an echo chamber for your voice. This helps to give your voice a fuller sound.

When you have a cold, the sinuses become blocked. A cold can make your voice sound deeper and more nasal.

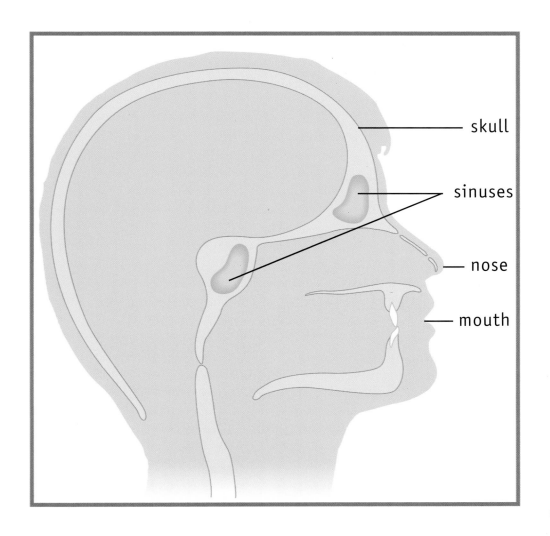

skull

sinuses

nose

mouth

Animal noses

Different animals have different types of noses. Whales and frogs have noses that are only small holes. Elephants have a long trunk for a nose. It is used to smell, drink water, communicate, and carry food to the mouth.

Some animals have a far better sense of smell than humans. The bloodhound is a type of dog that hunts by scent alone. It can follow a scent for more than 50 miles (80 kilometers).

Nose problems

Sometimes you cannot smell anything. This may be the result of a nose injury or a bad cold. It may also be caused by a small growth inside your nose that is blocking the nasal passages.

A cold is an infection of your nose and throat.

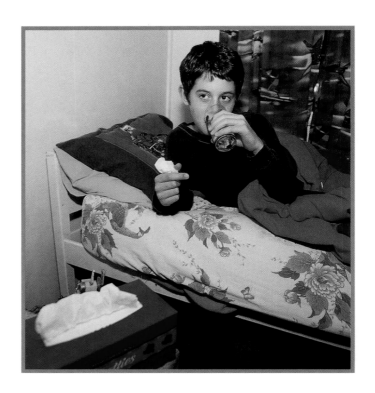

Colds

When you get a cold, tiny blood vessels in your nasal passages become swollen. The mucous tissues make more mucus. This causes liquid to run out of your nose. That is why you sneeze and blow your nose when you have a cold.

Allergies

Allergies can also cause your nasal passages to swell. People can be allergic to flowers, grass, dust, certain foods, cat or dog hair, and many other things.

Some people are allergic to pollution in the air.

Strong smells such as chopped onion can also cause your nasal passages to swell and your eyes to water. When you cry, tears drain into tear ducts in your nose.

Nose bleeds

The mucous tissues in your nasal passages are lined with many small blood vessels. When it is cold outside, the tissues become very dry and fragile.

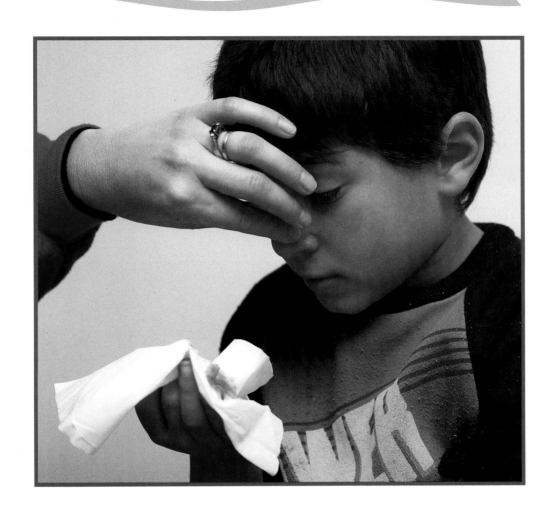

If you are struck on the nose, the blood vessels can break and cause a nosebleed. A cold can also dry out the mucous tissues and start a nosebleed.

Nose care

Dust and small particles that enter your nose can cause infections. A cold or allergies can also create a stuffy nose and breathing problems. These conditions can be treated by a doctor.

Sun protection

Your nose can easily get sunburned, so you should try to protect it from the sun. It is a good idea to wear a hat with a broad brim. Sunscreens can also help to prevent sunburn.

Nose injuries

The bones in your nose are very thin. If you break your nose, it can cause breathing problems. The nose is broken more often than any other part of the human body.

If you break your nose, you may need surgery to straighten it.

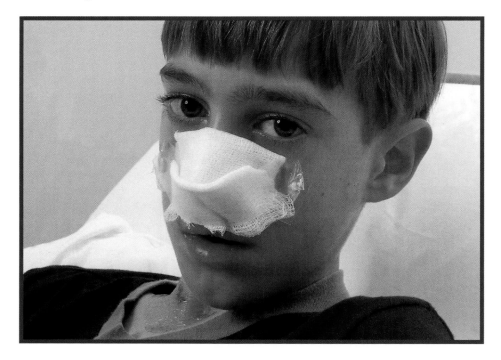

Your nose can be broken or damaged when you play sports such as hockey or football. It is important to wear a helmet with a face mask to protect your nose.

Nose surgery

Sometimes people are born with crooked bones in their noses. This can cause breathing problems that can be fixed by surgery.

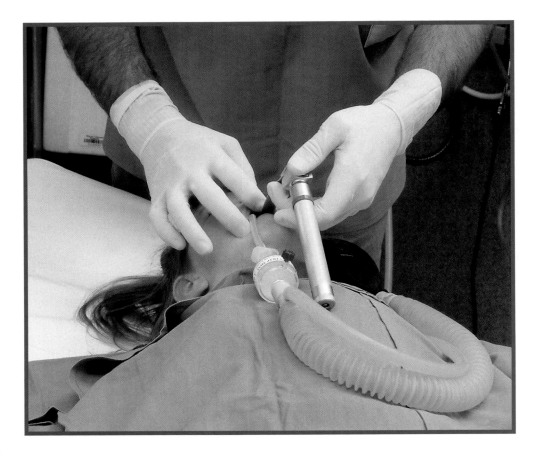

Glossary

allergies   a sensitivity to certain substances that often causes sneezing

elastic tissues   tissues that are movable and spring back into shape when moved

mucous tissues   tissues in the nose that produce mucus

mucus   thick, slimy liquid in the nose

nerves   fibers that carry messages from the brain to other parts of the body

Index

DATE			